Narcissism

A Comprehensive And Methodical Manual Outlining Effective And Verified Techniques For Women To Overcome Narcissism And Transform Their Behaviour

(Understanding The Intricacies Of Narcissism)

Jean-Philippe Gosselin

TABLE OF CONTENT

Effect On Interpersonal Relationships 1

Is It Better For You To Stay Or Go? 12

Understanding The Range Of Narcissistic Conduct 34

The Narcissistic Parent In The Family 58

Handling Anger 92

How Do Victims Of Narcissism Get Selected? 115

Dynamics In Which The Narrator Is A Parent Or An Authority Figure 136

Effect On Interpersonal Relationships

Let's connect this to interpersonal connections now. You may come across someone with these features more frequently if you live in a society that accepts narcissistic behavior in general. Establishing healthy relationships might be particularly difficult because narcissists frequently aim for positions of control and power.

Conversely, you may still come across narcissistic people in societies that detest such traits, but people in these communities may be more likely to identify and deal with them.

What precisely can you do then? It can be empowering to understand these cultural influences. It enables you to see that other people are participating in your experiences and interactions in addition to you and the narcissist. The greater cultural backdrop has an impact on them as well.

Difficult questions: How do you perceive narcissistic behavior depending on your cultural background and the culture in which you live?

Are there any societal standards or conventions that might have unintentionally promoted or permitted narcissistic behavior in your life?

In conclusion, a critical first step in your quest for self-awareness and the removal of toxic relationships is realizing the impact that power dynamics and cultural hierarchies have on narcissism. It gives you the confidence to face these obstacles head-on by reassuring you that you're not the only one. Recall that self-awareness is frequently the first step towards improving oneself, and this understanding of cultural influences is a useful tool in that process.

The way that narcissism is presented and handled can also be influenced by cultural norms surrounding gender roles. For example, in societies where gender roles are still prevalent, narcissism in men may be more acceptable, while narcissism in women may be frowned upon or stigmatized.

What are the potential cultural reactions to narcissistic traits?

Social sanctions: People who exhibit narcissistic features may be subject to social sanctions or exclusion in cultures where these traits are viewed as harmful to societal cohesion. These penalties can be in the form of formal reprimands or social seclusion, among other things.

Coping strategies: Cultures frequently have their strategies to deal with selfish people. This can involve utilizing customs and rituals to uphold social order, asking elders or other authorities for mediation, or communicating indirectly.

Cultural interventions: Several cultures may have developed special interventions to counter narcissistic behavior. Family, community, or religious leaders may work with the individual in these interventions to promote more socially acceptable behavior.

Cultural fusion and globalization: The globalization of communication and media has led to a blurring of cultural barriers. Particularly in urban, cosmopolitan settings, this can result in conflicts between more Westernised perspectives on narcissism and traditional cultural reactions.

Comprehending the various ways in which many cultures perceive and react to narcissistic qualities is an intricate and subtle undertaking. Historical and social settings, cultural norms and values, and other factors greatly influence these reactions. As they investigate these processes further, cultural psychologists can offer insight into the ways that narcissism is both a universal human feature and a phenomenon that is dependent on culture. This knowledge can promote effective communication and cross-cultural empathy in a globalized society.

Social Norms and Structures

Social norms and institutions are fundamental in determining how people behave individually and as a group. Acceptance or rejection of selfish behavior is one area where this influence is most noticeable. Characteristics of narcissism, which is a psychological trait that can range from healthy to malignant. Many social, historical, and cultural elements interact in a complicated way to shape how society perceives and deals with selfish behavior.

There are differences in the levels of tolerance for narcissistic behavior among nations and cultures. Individualism and self-promotion may be encouraged in some societies, which is consistent with narcissistic tendencies. On the other hand, collectivist societies might place more value on modesty and peace within the society, discouraging narcissistic impulses. Major role in determining how common and acceptable narcissistic behavior is in a certain community.

Historical patterns might also have an impact on the acceptance of narcissistic behavior. For instance, society may be more accepting of narcissistic qualities during times of economic prosperity and stability since achievement and self-promotion are frequently rewarded. On the other hand, cultures may value qualities like empathy and cooperation during times of crisis or social unrest, which could result in a rejection of narcissistic behavior. Historical events and cultural experiences can shape collective ideals and norms.

Social media, television, and film are examples of mass media that significantly influence society's norms and values. The presentation of narcissistic individuals as either heroes or villains might influence popular attitudes. For instance, a popular TV show featuring a narcissistic protagonist may inadvertently contribute to the acceptance of narcissistic conduct, especially among younger generations.

Societal conventions around narcissism sometimes begin in the family unit. Families emphasizing empathy, humility, and cooperation are more likely to generate individuals rejecting narcissistic characteristics. Conversely, families that promote rivalry, achievement, and self-centeredness may contribute to the acceptability of narcissistic behavior.

Gender standards can overlap with cultural attitudes about narcissistic behavior. In many civilizations, boldness and self-promotion are more socially acceptable in men than women. Women who demonstrate narcissistic qualities may encounter harsher censure and backlash compared to their male counterparts. This gender bias can affect how society views and tolerates narcissistic behavior.

Our investigation of negotiating narcissism among different cultures, individual personalities, and societal norms. As we've walked through numerous cultural lenses, it has become obvious that narcissism emerges differently across the world, influenced by a complex network of historical, social, and psychological elements. Understanding and understanding narcissism across varied cultural contexts is a key step toward building empathy, communication, and cooperation in our increasingly interconnected global society.

In the following chapter, we will analyze the worldwide landscape of narcissism, analyzing the broad patterns and difficulties that transcend boundaries. By zooming out from the microcosm of cultural variations, we shall acquire a broader perspective on the repercussions of narcissism on a global scale.

Is It Better For You To Stay Or Go?

Now, spend some time analyzing every narcissistic relationship you have ever experienced. List all the reasons you choose to stay with them and how being in that relationship has helped you grow under each. Make a case for why you ought to continue in those partnerships. Above all, examine closely who you were and who you are today compared to who you were.

Consider whether you are being true to yourself if you have decided to stay in a narcissistic relationship. An intriguing thing happens when a narcissist connects with an authentic and genuine individual. That's why I'm asking you if you're being your most authentic self. In today's society, the word "authenticity" is often utilized, but what exactly does it mean? Authenticity: what is it? Those that accept and love themselves for who they are are considered authentic. They don't take things personally as a result. They don't make things more personal.

Those who have experienced their fair share of trauma or difficulties are considered authentic. However, these are the kinds of people who keep going despite the difficulties they have met. They let themselves be vulnerable without worrying about what other people will think of them or if they will be judged for it. This authenticity makes you self-assured and values your viewpoint so much that you don't give much weight to what other people think.

That is to say when your true self meets the narcissist, it will be as if your strategy is knowledge. You are not going to succumb to manipulative strategies and egotistical behaviors. The narcissist becomes extremely irritated at you for not falling into any of their traps. It is uncomfortable for narcissists to be around real people. Being authentic will enable you to respond to the narcissist's grandiosity without fully engaging in their self-centeredness. You will listen, recognize, and then move on to the next topic without giving in to their arrogance.

Unfortunately, those who stay in narcissistic relationships tend to lose their genuineness. And if you choose to stay with a narcissist, it is among the things you need to consider. Consider who you wish to be instead of what you are or will become after years of suffering from narcissistic abuse. If you are prepared to embrace the right perspective to handle a narcissistic relationship in a way that won't negatively impact your mental or emotional health, examine it and be honest with yourself.

If you decide to stay, you must embrace and learn to appreciate who you are, even if being in such a relationship can be scary. Not every time will the narcissist believe. They won't accept your reality or validate you. They'll act in the exact opposite way. Thus, you must be self-possessed and validate yourself. It must be sufficient that you be aware of the truth about what is going on. Your knowledge is sufficient. You need to have a strong mindset and engage in constructive self-talk.

It's not always necessary for you to defend or explain yourself. Speak your truth to confirm yourself, not to please your spouse. Being honest and open-minded eliminates the narcissist's ability to manipulate others. You must be indifferent to what others say and believe if you want to be real. You must be content with who you are. You have to learn to recognize when to remove yourself from the situation and be unaffected by the narcissist to avoid tolerating or encouraging their harmful tendencies. Return gracefully and courteously. You will take away the narcissist's ability to control you by doing this.

Once you recognize manipulation and know how to react, you will find it impossible for others to manipulate. You have to reach a self-actualization point where you are aware of who you are and have congruency within. What impact will the narcissist have on you? Indeed. Being human means that you will experience hardships in life and that people you trust will hurt you. To navigate your narcissistic relationship, keep in mind your goals and your identity. Take care of yourself so that the narcissist's whipping doesn't alter who you are.

Acquire grace in your interactions and focus on your personal growth. You decide to continue being yourself and focus on your healing no matter what. To become resistant, be true to yourself and pay less attention to what the narcissist says. The best way to develop resistance is to esteem and give ourselves credit. We give narcissists too much credit, which is why they have such power over us. We nearly place an undue emphasis on their ideas and opinions.

Above all, guard your heart and your thoughts. The majority of your time is spent in your mind. You have to constantly cleanse your thoughts of all the poison that narcissistic backlash has to offer. The aim is to be healthy in body, mind, soul, and spirit. Numerous circumstances will arise in life. Difficulties will strengthen and fortify you. Additionally, you will get wiser from your exposure to narcissists when you recognize their behaviors and know how to react to them.

Though it's wonderful that we live in a time of self-improvement, we also need to recognize the significance of developing our spiritual selves and taking good care of our mental health. Do you or have you been married to a narcissist? If so, it's time to address your emotional health. You are sufficient and valuable. It's time to go inward and consider who you are. You will get increasingly resilient to the narcissist as you go along the path of self-love.

One should begin with self-discovery if they are insecure and lack self-awareness. You cannot value who you are and ask for respect because of all the insecurities you are dealing with. Learn to pay attention to your gut instinct and follow your intuition. Take action if anything doesn't feel quite right. React wisely, pausing to consider your options before taking action.

This life you lead is merely transitory. Every day you wake up is a day less of life, not a day more than you are given. As you approach the point at which your time on this planet is running out, what will you do with it? Are you going to let emotional abuse control your life because you are codependent and don't think well of yourself? Can you advocate for yourself, start the healing process, and have the bravery to struggle for the life you want?

Your moment of delight and joy must begin since time is running out. You are your hero and the person that will take you out of your current situation. Regain control and live and grow instead of just getting by! You deserve happiness, love, kindness, compassion, and comprehension. Your responsibility is to start providing for yourself if your partner cannot meet those demands. Extend yourself mercy and grace. And remember that you are strong, and all it takes to achieve your goals is self-empowerment!

Release yourself and put your needs first. We are still writing your narrative. You're simply in a difficult chapter. Now is the perfect moment to start over and motivate yourself to pursue transformation and change. Remorse or suffering shouldn't stop you from pursuing your goals or cause you to turn around.

Chapter 5: Handling Narcissistic Personality Disorder: A Guide

You do have options if you believe you suffer from narcissistic personality disorder. You have the chance and capacity to take control of your life and properly treat this widespread condition, even though it can be challenging. You have actions that you can take to support those around you and yourself. You can improve your life by doing these things and accepting responsibility for your actions.

You must first recognize and acknowledge an issue with how you interact with the outside world. You can try to act in more socially acceptable ways after you acknowledge that you have a narcissistic personality. You must understand your identity and behavior.

This can be accomplished by sitting down and listing the self-defeating, damaging, or maladaptive behaviors you participate in. Recognize the habits that are bringing you the most trouble in your life. Make another list of the actions you take that are beneficial and constructive or productive after that. It is advisable to attempt to avoid the behaviors on the first list and try more of the ones on the second.

Next, you must be prepared to discipline yourself for the actions on the first list. What steps can you take to deter yourself from acting in this way? Put these things in writing; you must be prepared to act on them when you catch yourself doing bad things.

Conversely, enumerate commendable incentives or awards for participating in the adaptive activities. Reward yourself with anything from your second list whenever you behave properly and appropriately. Rewards and negative reinforcement are used to teach people what is and is not acceptable. If you're willing to do so, you can alter your behavior by becoming conscious of your behavioral reactions and adapting your replies accordingly.

The secret is consistently giving yourself positive reinforcement and negative reinforcers for specific activities. You must always perform this task. To implement such rewards and penalties, you must be willing to examine your actions objectively. If you can, you should encourage yourself to participate in constructive activities and reduce the frequency of your problems and actions. You can accomplish these tasks independently or with a therapist's guidance. You could also get assistance from any loved one in your life to make these kinds of behavioral changes. Finding positive and negative reinforcers for you, as well as learning which behaviors are problematic and which are not, can be greatly aided by a therapist.

Nonetheless, you can significantly alter your life if you are prepared to acknowledge that you have a problem and to keep an eye on your actions. Your life should get easier, and you will get along with people better. However, you can't lower your defenses. Regrettably, NPD is widespread and incurable. However, you can manage your habits and have a far better life if you work hard.

Your NPD can be managed with treatment and potentially medication to treat co-occurring mental health issues. For instance, anti-anxiety medications can assist in managing the anxiety that is related to your illness. Remain optimistic, as you are in charge of your destiny. It is up to you to decide to do the right things and lead a better life.

Chapter 1: Exposing Selfishness

Describe the characteristics and personality of narcissism.

A persistent grandiosity pattern, an insatiable need for admiration, and a lack of empathy for other people define the complex psychological construct known as narcissistic traits and personality. These people, who are sometimes called narcissists, have a strong feeling of self-importance that goes beyond typical self-assurance. Investigating the essential characteristics that characterize this unique psychological profile is necessary to understand the essence of narcissistic personality.

An exaggerated sense of self is the fundamental component of narcissistic personalities. Overconfidence in one's skills, accomplishments, and abilities is a common trait among narcissists. This grandiosity frequently shows itself as an endless need for approval and attention from other people. They think of themselves as remarkable and deserving of special attention; therefore, they strive for admiration and acclaim. This ongoing need for external validation shapes their relationships and behaviors, which becomes a motivating factor in their interactions and decisions. The absence of empathy is a hallmark of a narcissistic personality. Narcissists find it difficult to empathize with or comprehend the feelings of others because they are too preoccupied with taking care of themselves. A disrespect for the sentiments and welfare of people around them may result from this emotional detachment. Even though they could be charming and charismatic, this is usually not a sign of sincere concern but rather a means to an end—a technique to control people.

Under the surface of assurance and self-assurance, narcissists frequently struggle with low self-esteem. Ironically, there is a fragility beneath their opulent veneer. Intense reactions, ranging from defensiveness to aggressiveness, might be triggered by criticism or perceived threats to their sense of self. Because of how brittle their self-esteem is, they constantly seek affirmation from others to support their sense of value.

Narcissistic people often fantasize about having limitless wealth, power, attractiveness, or the perfect partner. As a coping strategy, these imaginations offer people an escape from the truth of their limitations. An idealized self-image can be an enticing force that pushes someone to pursue objectives that may be impractical or motivated by a need for unwavering praise.

The narcissistic personality trait of exploitative inclinations is another characteristic. Narcissists may take advantage of people for their benefit without feeling regret or guilt. This can take many forms, such as manipulating relationships, preying on others' weaknesses, and the detriment of others around them. Frequently, they prioritize their interests over moral issues.

It might be difficult to build and sustain connections with selfish people. Their interpersonal interactions are frequently characterized by a lack of true connection, notwithstanding their apparent appeal. They may find it difficult to build genuine, mutually beneficial connections because most interactions are transactional and focus on meeting their wants.

Understanding the interaction between grandiosity, a lack of empathy, a fixation with idealized dreams, exploitative impulses, and fragile self-esteem is necessary to define narcissistic traits and personality. Understanding these traits is essential to managing relationships with people who exhibit narcissistic traits and promoting a greater understanding of the complexity ingrained in their mental health.

Understanding The Range Of Narcissistic Conduct

There is a continuum of narcissistic behavior that includes a variety of expressions that differ in severity and style. Understanding this spectrum is essential to comprehend the variety of ways that narcissistic tendencies can appear in people. Understanding the range of narcissistic behavior enables a more nuanced comprehension of these intricate characteristics, ranging from mild inclinations to more apparent patterns.

On the milder end of the scale, some people may exhibit narcissistic qualities that don't interfere as much with their relationships and everyday activities. These could include a sporadic need for approval, affirmation, or an increased emphasis on one's accomplishments. In certain situations, the characteristics might not significantly impact the person's capacity to build positive relationships or engage in reciprocal interactions. Nonetheless, to stop these inclinations from developing into more problematic conduct, one must be conscious of them.

As one moves along the spectrum, more signs of mild narcissistic behavior appear. This group has a more regular pattern of self-centeredbehavior and may use subtle manipulations to uphold their idealized self-concept. They may have trouble showing empathy and putting their needs before others. Even if their actions might not be blatantly harmful, they could make it difficult to build genuine relationships and even fuel interpersonal disputes.

People in the intermediate range frequently exhibit a continuous craving for approval from others. This may result in a never-ending need for approval and attention and an increased susceptibility to slights or criticism. They may respond defensively to preserve their self-perception since their self-worth is still brittle. Acknowledging these characteristics becomes crucial when managing relationships with people who could exhibit erratic behaviors ranging from charming to defensive.

Narcissistic conduct gets increasingly destructive and disruptive as it moves toward the severe end of the scale. These people have a strong sense of entitlement and take advantage of others for their gain without feeling guilty. Their relationships become centered upon manipulation, and to stay in power, they could employ emotional abuse or gaslighting. There is a marked lack of genuine empathy in favor of a deliberate emphasis on accomplishing their goals, frequently at the expense of others.

At the end of the range, selfish people can be extremely harmful and toxic in relationships. Their lack of regret, along with their exploitation tendencies, can cause serious harm to people around them. Identifying these behaviors is vital for those attempting, as well as for professionals in mental health and counseling disciplines who may be working with clients impacted by extreme narcissistic personalities.

In conclusion, it is important to comprehend the range of selfish behavior, which extends from minor characteristics to more extreme patterns. Understanding these differences helps people navigate relationships more intelligently, and it allows experts to customize interventions based on the particular ways that narcissistic tendencies appear. Recognizing the intricacy of the spectrum allows society to cultivate a more understanding and considerate strategy for handling the difficulties presented by narcissistic persons.

Chapter 9: Recuperation

I firmly believe in the ability of self-healing and that self-care and healing techniques can eventually address any level of emotional suffering. You may, to a significant extent, move past the experience of narcissistic abuse if you have the right support and belief in yourself. It may be a long path and undoubtedly not be simple. Even the most detrimental emotional events can be overcome to move on and have a healthy, fulfilling life that is emotionally secure, even though the effects may not completely disappear. This occurs due to the brain's amazing ability to rewire itself, replacing old, harmful thought cycles with new, healthy ones and teaching the body and mind how to live and love again.

Get yourself a nice new journal, or grab an old one first. Numerous abuse survivors can vouch for the effectiveness of merely putting your sentiments in writing and processing them verbally. You may still be processing or trying to make sense of a lot of the details of your encounters with narcissistic abuse. Recall that the crucial aspect of this situation is to avoid concentrating on deciphering or solving your abuser's psychological tricks. Here, the main goal should be to process your emotions and separate the bad emotions from the cognitive patterns causing them. For instance, you might have overheard your abuser accuse you of being either too thin or too obese all the time. After writing about how this affected you, reaffirm that there is nothing physically wrong with you and that this was only one of your abuser's many manipulative techniques. Allowing these emotions to continuously hurt you is essentially giving your abuser your surrender. Positive, affirming thoughts about your amazing body and all that it has accomplished for you should replace these negative ones. Gratitude expressions can also effectively remove emotions of emptiness and worthlessness. Once more, it won't instantly make all your bad emotions disappear. It takes time to develop constructive mental patterns, but the effort is worth it. Keep your future ideas free from negativity from your previous connection.

Exercise or contemplative movement therapy, such as yoga, are alternative ways to help you process and let go of unpleasant emotions and release this energy. Numerous yoga poses are made expressly to assist you in shifting your mental focus from unfavorable feelings into a more optimistic area. Fostering a sound physical state always promotes sound mental and cognitive patterns.

Never hesitate to seek out outside assistance. Being able to rely on people for support will be crucial, particularly in the initial weeks or months after a painful emotional experience. Maybe the abuse you suffered at the hands of a narcissist caused you to become estranged from friends and/or relatives. It's time to get back in touch with those you love. Be not afraid. They won't even ask you for specifics because they will likely be happy to see you again. Just accept their love and support and draw on it when necessary. To help you process and get past the specifics of your abuse, ask to talk about some of the details when you're ready.

It will be crucial for you to educate yourself about narcissists and their strategies if you wish to protect yourself from abusers in the future. You might need to work on putting up barriers and waiting for people to show you they are trustworthy if you feel too eager to trust in your last relationship. This could be challenging for individuals who are emotionally and naturally giving. Although this might be an incredible quality, it's vital to remember that not everyone you encounter will be well-intentioned. I hope you never have to encounter another narcissist. However, it won't hurt to be aware of how to recognize one should one come your way and steer clear of that influence.

These are two of the most crucial things you can do to ensure your success on the road to recovery. It won't be simple to ignore these emotions, particularly if you've heard someone tell you that you're not smart or good enough or have some other problem for months or years. Moving past this will take time, but it's crucial to develop a daily routine of mentally or verbally asserting that you are a survivor of narcissistic abuse and that you were resilient enough to escape.

In this process, meditation can be a very useful technique. First, find a comfortable place to sit that is distraction-free and silent. Take deep breaths each time you inhale, and practice breathing gently. As you breathe, pay attention to your body in space and experience every element of it. If you would like, you can create your tiny mantra or choose from various guided meditations that are accessible online. Regardless of what you choose to do, try to set aside some time every day to concentrate on your assertion. Repeat the words out slowly, several times to yourself. Remind yourself that you are strong, that you are enough, that you are cherished, and that you accept and love yourself. Just repeating these sentences to yourself will start to dissolve the negative thought patterns and bad habits that used to trouble you and make you anxious. You will eventually reach a point where the intrusive ideas causing your bad emotions will vanish from your memory. Positive thoughts will gradually replace these negative ones as you practice, and it will start to feel more automatic. For those who have never meditated before, it may seem a bit unusual. Still, if you are having trouble breaking free from those negative, repetitive thinking patterns, I strongly recommend trying it.

Lastly, make every effort to develop a regular sleep plan that allows you to sleep for at least eight hours each night. You may find that meditating briefly each night before bed helps your brain wind down and get ready for sleep. Try to go to bed simultaneously every night and engage in a relaxing activity right before. Avoid eating junk food late at night, which can keep you awake longer and cause sleep disturbances.

Recognize that you are not alone in your suffering and that you are strong enough to overcome this horrifying trauma. Reaffirm every day that you are worth the effort to become well—remember to love and care for yourself.

In the unlikely event that your abuser reappears in your life, arm yourself. Establish clear limits and a policy of no communication at all. Do not answer phone calls, texts, or anything. There is nothing good that he can provide you, and he is not worth it. You are no longer affected by that.

Examining a Narcissist's Feelings

It's a popular misperception that narcissists have no emotions. This is untrue. They frequently experience feelings of shame, hatred, envy, and loneliness. They are good at hiding their emotions from others and avoiding and dodging them. It is sometimes described as an extreme and forced form of stoicism. Rather than depending on others, they rely on their sense of specialness to keep up their act.

Compassion

One of the most common emotional problems linked to narcissism is a lack of empathy. People who lack narcissism typically come naturally with some degree of empathy. Additionally, it is possible to develop one's empathy. Empathy is summed up in the proverb, "Take a walk in their shoes."

A narcissist is incapable of developing empathy, nor can they even attempt to do so. They don't know how to use it and don't comprehend it. The narcissist may become enraged when someone in their immediate vicinity demonstrates empathy for someone else because they are not the center of attention.

Envy

One of the main emotions felt by narcissists is jealousy. They think of themselves as superior and strive to be the greatest. Envy arises when someone emerges who is genuinely superior at something. Take this group of males who are playing hoops. Although it is only human to want to be the best, most people eventually learn to accept when a different player is superior. For the narcissist, though, this is not feasible. This may cause the superior person to experience severe jealousy.

Disgrace

Narcissists can feel humiliated anytime their grandiose illusions are questioned or when someone else is demonstrated to be more skilled in a particular area.

They may grow enraged as a result and attack the persons who they believe have degraded them.

Being alone

The narcissist may feel extremely alone if the focus is turned elsewhere. This holds even if there are other people around them. They value attention and adoration highly, so they may feel unwelcome and alone when they don't get much of it.

Fury

One of the most frequent feelings that a narcissist feels is anger. If the person cannot control anger, it may turn into rage. The slightest things, like a friend taking two minutes to talk to someone else while they are nearby, might cause someone to lose their temper. Anger can be sparked by anything that diverts a narcissist's attention. Intimidation, condemnation, envy, or rage can also incite a narcissist to become enraged.

Feeling of envy

The narcissist believes they deserve the best of everything and that everything they own is the best. They may get jealous, for example, if they see someone driving a finer or newer car. This jealousy can occasionally become almost compulsive. They will give it all their attention, consider it frequently, and attempt to outdo whoever owns what they are jealous of in many ways.

Lack of fullness

Another emotion that is often associated with narcissism is emptiness. It can give them a queasy or disturbed feeling. Keep in mind that the narcissist must believe they are strong and the center of attention. The emptiness may begin to appear when things are not occurring. This may lead them to take action, such as disparaging the person now receiving attention, to refocus attention on themselves.

Joy

They genuinely don't experience happiness. Rather, people often confuse the happiness from feeling powerful with the true happiness from not being a narcissist. For instance, when someone lands the new job of their dreams, they are grateful for the chance to start over. But happiness is more of a sense of power and the belief that landing that job will improve their status for a narcissist.

Do Others Face Danger from Narcissists?

Although narcissism is undoubtedly bad, it can go far deeper than what is written in textbooks. Those who are close to a narcissist may not be aware that they are in danger since the harm is typically psychological rather than physical. If injury is done, it is typically emotional and may take longer to manifest or take its toll.

The emotions or welfare of those around a narcissist is unimportant to them. When they strike out, they do not intend to inflict physical or emotional harm. All they're doing is protecting the self-image they're attempting to project. For instance, someone might reveal they received a promotion at a party. Everyone, except the narcissist, congratulates the person on this joyful development. Instead of expressing gratitude to the person, the narcissist could try to disparage them because they are displeased that they are the focus of attention. In this case, they aim to draw attention back to themselves rather than make the other person feel worse.

At first, the emotional damage inflicted by a narcissist may not seem like much. But with time, the effects may worsen to the point that the victim's happiness and sense of self-worth decline. This is particularly true if the narcissist happens to be the person's close friend, family member, or romantic partner because of how highly valued their treatment and viewpoint are.

For example, a man and a woman are dating. He is conceited. At first, his clinging to authority and attention may seem a little irritating. But as time passes, he begins to make fun of her when he thinks she has achieved something that he hasn't or when he sees her talking to someone else when they are together. It can be quite emotionally taxing to receive this treatment from someone you love.

Recall that parental abuse of this kind can have serious and enduring impacts, as it is one of the hypotheses as to why someone becomes a narcissist.

You cannot change the narcissist, and he cannot be a sincere friend. There are good reasons for some people to stay in contact with the narcissist. You must establish limits to live and prevent abuse. To learn how to handle the narcissist, see Chapter 5.

The Narcissistic Parent In The Family

Children of narcissistic parents face special challenges because, typically, they are not aware of the problem until they are older and struggling to resolve it on their own. Many become aware that their parents are narcissists only after they have grown up and are finding it difficult to repair the harm that has been done to them. Because this is the picture they provide to the outer world, narcissistic parents appear to be the ideal parents. Regretfully, the kids endure silent suffering.

They enhance their image by using their kids.

Narcissistic parents, like all narcissists, have extremely low self-esteem and use their kids as a means of achieving their unfulfilled ambitions. They overindulge, expecting their kids to be flawless, and worry about others taking advantage of their flaws. Because their parents had been living through them their entire lives, the children also, as a result, lose their sense of identity and become estranged from their own needs and desires.

With their kids, they are frugal, but not with themselves.

They will shame their children for articulating their demands. The kids eventually learn to give in to the narcissist, which makes them easy pickings. They learn early on that they are not worthy of the goods to which they are entitled.

They set up rivalries between their kids. This is how a narcissistic parent gets their kids to be loyal to them. They manipulate others by showing favoritism and setting them against one another to satisfy their demands. The parents smother the child they believe has excellent traits because they detest the child who represents their shortcomings. The siblings don't grow up feeling hatred toward one another.

They don't recognize their kids as unique people.

They ignore boundaries and invade their children's privacy because they consider their kids to be nothing more than extensions of themselves. They read their emails or letters, tell them what to dress, meddle in their personal affairs, and treat them with complete contempt.

They make their kids play roles or take on duties that are too big for them.

With their kids, the parents play the victim role, making the kids behave more like their parents or spouse than like kids. As long as their demands are satisfied, the narcissistic parent doesn't give a damn about how bad this can be for the kid.

They never offer an apology.

They'll never take responsibility for their errors or apologize to their kids. It will never be their fault; it will always be someone else's. To protect their reputation, they won't think twice about lying or ruining the reputation of their kids. Despite being the ideal parents, they would portray their kids as wicked and unappreciative.

Kids with narcissistic parents must get expert assistance. Along with trying to mend fences with their siblings, they also need to comprehend what turned their parents into narcissists. The kids should get therapy and relocate to a secure environment if their narcissistic parent is abusing them.

The Selfish Partner

Sees you as an ever-flowing source of narcissistic sustenance.

You ought to anticipate his needs before he ever asks. You are expected to provide devotion and support whenever needed. The narcissist will never give anything back; therefore, you will have to give until you are empty. Expect narcissistic anger if he feels that your supply has run out.

He is excessively envious.

They don't want anything to go in the way of the constant supply of their fix since you are it. If they are envious of anything and everyone, even your father, your siblings, your kids, and the family pet, don't be shocked.

Projects all of his shortcomings or bad qualities onto you.

You will be labeled as needy and ungrateful by the narcissist. He'll say you're unreasonable and greedy. He's the only one who says as much, though. He might call you names like flirtatious, sloppy, liar, or cheater—all of which reflect his actions. Naturally, the narcissist believes he is perfect.

Makes you angry.

He'll act in this way in an attempt to get you to leave. The narcissist saw this as validation of his long-held suspicion—or rather, fear—that you would leave him. Additionally, he can turn it against you by feigning victimization.

If he knows you will urge him to stay, he can also be the one to threaten to leave.

Silently treats you.

Without explaining, he will do this to torment you. It's a traditional passive-aggressive abuse technique. It's his tactic for taking charge and knocking you down without saying anything. He'll act like nothing occurred and expect you to accept him without any argument later.

Has affairs and is flirtatious.

It's a result of his ravenous and persistent demand for approval. He can't help but get excited about finding a new love. Because of his skewed perception of himself, he believes that flirtation is happening between him and even amiable women.

Has a porn addiction.

Because porn is another readily available narcissistic supply, many narcissists also tend to become hooked to it. Additionally, they may find it easy to control individuals through internet relationships.

Abuses you.

He might mistreat you physically, psychologically, sexually, or emotionally. The intention behind this abuse is to control you and make sure you never stop giving a narcissistic supply. The narcissist has always been pursuing your supply; in actuality, he is not in love with you.

Apologizes and hopes that everything will return to normal.

This is another nasty method. Interestingly, he expects things to return to normal instantly, even though his expression of regret may or may not be genuine. However, he may condition you so you'll immediately accept him without hesitation.

It is conceivable, but unlikely, for the narcissist to change. Seeing a specialist can help anyone with a narcissistic spouse choose whether or not it's wise to continue the relationship. It's typically preferable to leave.

Chapter 6: Self-Understanding Techniques for Managing the Seas of Selfishness

Greetings from this latest leg of our self-discovery trip, fearless reader. The final chapter takes us into the narcissist's head, where we find ourselves adrift in the choppy seas of self-obsession and occasionally in dark, uncomfortable surroundings. But why is it crucial to sail across these waters? Why set out on this journey to discover who you are?

Being aware of oneself is the first step toward living a whole and genuine life. Thus, the answer is both straightforward and incredibly intricate. We can get caught in cycles of self-obsession and self-deception, adrift in a sea of paradoxes and confusions, if we don't have a firm grasp on who we are and our thought and behavior patterns.

Thus, ask yourself: are you aware of who you are, what drives you, what worries you, what you want, or do you often find yourself aimlessly cruising the choppy seas of self-centeredness? If so, you should read this chapter. Here, we'll provide the resources you need to overcome these challenges and start along the road to a more profound and fulfilling understanding of yourself.

One of the basic tenets of self-understanding, self-awareness, will be our starting point for this journey. The knowledge and comprehension of oneself, encompassing our ideas, emotions, drives, convictions, and actions, is known as self-awareness. It is the capacity to turn within and examine our thoughts and emotions with objectivity and criticism.

In a world fixed on appearance, self-awareness is sometimes undervalued but is one of the most potent abilities we can develop. As the ancient Greek philosopher Socrates observed in the fifth century BC, "Know thyself." This adage is still applicable today. Understanding who we are helps us live more genuine and meaningful lives, better control our emotions, and make more educated decisions.

However, how can we develop this self-awareness? How do we start to uncover the true selves beneath the façades and personas we present to the outside world? We must investigate several methods and approaches that can help us become more self-aware and, in the end, steer clear of selfishness to find the answers to these concerns.

We must first develop our ability to observe. Observation is the root of self-awareness. We can start recognizing our thought patterns, pinpointing our emotions, and comprehending how these things affect our actions through observation. Additionally, practicing attentive self-observation is the ideal place to start.

To practice mindful self-observation, we must pause and become aware of our internal experiences at any given time. It involves pausing during our hectic daily schedules to become aware of our sensations and thoughts. Doing this allows us to recognize trends, spot limiting ideas, and learn how we lie to ourselves. However, how do you engage in conscious self-reflection? We encourage you to go more into this method in the upcoming sections of this chapter, as we will provide a useful strategy for developing self-awareness.

Now, let's discuss mindful self-observation in more detail. Starting this practice can be as simple as setting aside time each day to sit silently and watch your thoughts. At this point, attempt to observe your thoughts as an impartial observer. Don't judge them or try to change them; simply observe them. You'll notice that some ideas appear to stick with you while others come and go. Some might be comfortable, while others might not be. Some may seem random, while others may have a clear connection to what is going on in your life.

Do you recall the Gestalt therapy pioneer Fritz Perls' 1960s practice of looking up at a cloud in the sky? We can see our thoughts floating around like clouds traveling across the sky. This is essentially self-observation on a conscious level.

We can develop our self-awareness through other methods besides mindful self-observation. One of them is meditation. In "Full Catastrophe Living" (1990), Jon Kabat-Zinn described how meditation helps us connect with our "inner witness," the part of ourselves that can notice our thoughts and feelings without being overcome by them. We can develop a peaceful, focused awareness through meditation, a useful tool in pursuing self-awareness.

Another effective method for developing self-awareness is journaling. Writing down our feelings, ideas, and experiences helps us see connections and patterns we might miss. Writing can assist us in gaining a more detached and objective perspective on our experiences, which can help us accept and understand ourselves better.

What kind of things should I write in my reflective notebook, you might wonder? Writing down the ideas and emotions you have noticed throughout your attentive self-observation or meditation sessions is a good place to start. You can write about your aspirations, worries, and hopes. You can write about the people you've interacted with and the effects they've had on you. You can write about your worries and your hopes, about your triumphs and your setbacks.

Characteristics of the Targets

Emotional Frailty and Discretion

The Emotional Fragility: The Endless Secrets to Realizing and Embracing Your Self-Esteem

Emotional affectability and emotional delicacy are very different from one another. To a larger extent, affectability is a trait you could possess. Then, even more, delicacy is an inability to handle your most confusing inner moods. Therefore, being delicate means having difficulty enduring even the most minor daily adversities.

For a major explanation, we reviewed how those two terms differed. A lot of people try to make their emotional sensitivity uniform. They rationalize it by saying that it's just the way they are and how they continue living their lives. They usually say, "I can't change that; I'm just a sensitive individual."

Emotional finesse can often elicit debilitating feelings laden with tension, worry, and depression.

It's also crucial to understand that there is no room for forgiveness if your actions or mentality just cause you to feel helpless, aging, and without control over yourself. Not when all you get back is suffering. In essence, sensitive people see reality from a wider perspective. They are far more adept at negotiating with their demands and the environment in general. On the other hand, delicate people are emotionally limited.

Furthermore, this trait will typically be a sign of many more serious fundamental problems. We're talking about issues like debilitating disorders, anxiety, terrible emotional management, and so forth. For this reason, we should devote more time to examining this subject.

Emotional Fragility: Origins and Features

A few years ago, the American College Health Association published a fascinating study on emotional intelligence. They talked about a stressful metric in it: children nowadays have far higher rates of emotional dependence, stress, and misery. Finally, attempted suicide rates are also significantly higher in this age group. Beneath this measurement lies an emotional delicacy. There is a glaring shortage of resources to address even common problems.

A significant percentage of these mental health problems have childhood-related roots. Families from the last few decades have been unaware of the method by which the public has started to demand an ever-increasing amount of capabilities. Because of this, parents now have to put in a lot more effort to encourage their kids to think critically, even at such an early age.

They try to provide them with every resource possible to ensure they succeed. They push them to go above and beyond and constantly remind them of how unique they are and how they should develop properly. That's all that is reasonable. Either way, they're missing a few important details with that strategy.

The most important is that parents protect their children from disappointment. These kids also struggle with learning how to make decisions on their own. They experience insecurity and find it extremely difficult to control their own emotions. They gradually realize that they're not all that "uncommon" after all. They realize they lack the resources, tools, and tactics to address the most pressing problems.

We will look into the typical traits of emotionally sensitive people now.

How could I tell if I'm sensitive to emotions or not?

Some traits of emotionally sensitive people are as follows:

Incapacity to understand and process emotions such as anger, pity, frustration, and so on... They often overreact to these kinds of emotions.

A constant impression of nothingness.

Feeling overcome by trivial problems, discrepancies, or any situation that doesn't turn out how they had hoped.

Unable to control discontent.

Having trouble taking ownership of their own lives. It is a lot for them.

Ongoing problems in their social lives.Feeling that everyone in their vicinity has betrayed them or is a mistake.

Low energy levels, remoteness, persistent despondency.

They seem to be uneasy, taking on almost any task. Their self-esteem is poor, and they feel inadequate.

Occasionally, they react violently or angrily when things don't work out the way they had anticipated.

Your mental health often depends on your upbringing and the type of early relationships you have with other people. Either way, a toxic upbringing or little education doesn't spell doom. You can always overcome emotional delicacy with time.

Techniques for developing a strong sense of self and emotional stability:

Imagine a porcelain cup if you need to understand how to become emotionally solid. You understand how delicate it is. Even the prior breaks from when it was broken can be seen. That porcelain cup, though, is most definitely not delicate. Its shape, substance, and numerous small imperfections make it incredibly beautiful.

Generally speaking, you can allow yourself to be sensitive but not to be delicate. Strive to avoid crossing the line that splits you apart as a whole. Do not let your character, principles, or inner beauty escape you. But how would you go about doing that? How would you eliminate the sweetness that prevents you from feeling happy?

Being aware of your emotional weaknesses is the first step. We are talking about all the empty places that create problems and breakpoints. Although this may sound strange, studies have shown that such treatment can be effective. It's a fantastic way to use colors, canvases, and drawings to explore your thoughts, emotions, and inner concerns.

Assuming personal liability is the second stage. Delicate people believe that they are victims of their illness, of society, or other people. They never do anything but react, like a ball bouncing between two unyielding barriers. Instead of just reacting, you must assume command and demonstrate a sincere, audacious sense of accountability.

This responsibility also means letting go of the past and changing your life. Fear is a part of all progressions, but if you can get those pebbles out of the way of your daily existence, you'll notice how much more secure you've grown. Finally, you can take charge of your own life.

Lastly, we must emphasize that this is not an easy process. To go the entire route frequently requires the support of a good clinician. Remember that, despite how difficult it may appear, you usually have the chance to end up emotionally stable. It can transform your porcelain cup into an incredible, sturdy, and beautifully crafted object.

What techniques may I use because I work in HR?

Managing narcissism from your position calls for an organized and well-rounded strategy. The following organizational techniques and interventions might help lessen the detrimental consequences of narcissism in the workplace:

Establish an All-Inclusive Corporate Culture:

Encourage a collaborative, inclusive, and respectful workplace culture. Establish areas for candid dialogue and hearing every employee's viewpoint, ensuring no one's voice is silenced or unheard.

Educate People on the Signs of Narcissism:

Plan training sessions on narcissism awareness and its detrimental consequences on the workplace for all staff members. Staff awareness will increase, and resources for handling difficult circumstances will be provided.

Establish definite boundaries:

Set clear guidelines for appropriate workplace behavior at the individual and organizational levels. Ensure that the guidelines and expectations for interactions with leadership and coworkers are understood.

Promote constructive criticism:

Establish a setting where accepting and promoting constructive criticism is encouraged. Workers should be able to voice their opinions and concerns without worrying about facing consequences.

Encourage cooperation:

Promote teamwork among staff members by assigning them group projects and team-building exercises. This will foster a feeling of team spirit and lessen egotistical attitudes.

Provide Resources and Assistance for Emotional Health:

Provide tools for the mental health of your staff, such as stress management classes or psychological support services. An office culture that prioritizes employees' wellbeing fosters a robust and wholesome corporate culture.

Put into Practice Objective Vacation Management Protocols:

Establish transparent and objective vacation management policies to ensure that no worker is penalized or given preference due to the selfish actions of coworkers or managers.

Keep an eye on the climate within the organization:

Work environment surveys should be conducted regularly to gauge employee happiness and well-being. This will make it easier to spot any problems and enable prompt action.

Every Employee Should Be Respected:
Managers and leaders are responsible for setting an example of inclusive and polite behavior.

Handle Problems Right Away:
Deal with narcissistic situations as soon as they become problematic. Don't let inappropriate behavior continue; address problems as soon as possible.

Recall that combating narcissism in the workplace necessitates teamwork. The detrimental impacts of narcissism can be lessened, and a more upbeat and cooperative work environment for all employees can be created by putting into practice focused organizational interventions and encouraging a positive workplace culture.

Handling Anger

How can I get over my anger?

You must have asked yourself that question a million times. When you reach a stage where you are aware of what happened throughout your childhood, you will ask yourself this question.

You are aware of the fact that you were in an abusive relationship. You're upset with your egotistical mother for showing you hate rather than affection. You will be upset with your father for being unresponsive or absent. Occasionally, you will discover that your father participated in all of the maltreatment you endured during that period. You can even become enraged with your siblings for doing nothing but watching on.

Your fury has a purpose. On the one hand, it can aid in your comprehension of the circumstances surrounding your predicament. On the other hand, holding onto your anger indefinitely will only make matters worse for you. You simply don't need it right now when you're still attempting to heal.

We occasionally wear a mask of rage. Indeed, it is undoubtedly simpler to project an image of toughness and respond sharply to any intrusion into your personal life with a caustic remark.

Wearing this mask instead of the other is undoubtedly simpler. What other mask? It's the one that reveals your vulnerability, fear, and insecurity. Does that response sound like you? Yes, it's the same behavior or response as your narcissistic mother's—fake control and power on the outside but real helplessness on the inside.

You wouldn't initially associate your feelings of rage with your early life. Denying the whole truth is something that happens a lot. But you'll accept reality and understand the source of all that fury after introspection and soul-searching.

Gradual Recognition

When a daughter of a narcissistic mother discovers—and understands, of course—why Mother treated her in that manner, her anger toward her mother explodes. She starts to realize the effects of her treatment and attitude.

That takes some time to occur. The family feels like something is awry before they come to that realization. She senses something is wrong even at a young age, but she's not exactly sure what it is.

She would be living in a fantasy world. She will, in essence, continue to believe that her mother is acting in her best interests even while being mistreated. She might even start to question why she didn't measure up. If there is a brother in the family, she might even start to believe that she could hardly accomplish anything correctly because her brother seems to have everything figured out.

She will need considerable time to connect the dots before she can. When they eventually learn the truth and realize what happened, some women have already gotten married or are starting their careers.

She handled her circumstances, hoping to make things right, which is one aspect of her gradual realization. She was holding out hope that she might somehow make things normal. She detached herself from her pain after rationalizing her mother's actions. All of it is a misguided attempt to win her mother's affection.

Her universe collides with her growing awareness of the wrongs being done and her intense need for her mother's love. Naturally, cognitive dissonance results.

The Tipping Point

What will eliminate a daughter's cognitive dissonance is the following query. The solution is straightforward: she is beginning to realize what is happening. In a metaphorical sense, any cup you gently fill will eventually fill full. That's what occurs when a youngster grows up with a harsh mother who is narcissistic. She sort of gets tired of it. The abuse she endured has been heaped upon her; in this instance, it is already excessively excessive. Then, instead of requiring her mother's affection, she begins to survive her mother's brand of "loving."

The abuse completely changes her fight-or-flight response. Unfortunately, excessive use has almost eliminated the flight option this time. She is now prepared to defend herself; rage is a positive thing at this point. Her entire strategy of denial has now been abandoned. She was scared to confront her mother and the truth about her circumstances, but now she's prepared for a showdown.

Every Human Is Hardwired with It

Humans, indeed, have an innate tendency toward rage. It's a coping strategy we use. It's the feeling we let loose when we're eager to finish tasks quickly. Scholars refer to it as the stress reaction.

Unfortunately, there are two sides to this fight-or-flight reaction. On the one hand, it allows you to accomplish things you might not have otherwise done. Conversely, it is a condition that impairs our capacity for rational thought.

Scientists have examined how rage affects people. Physically, you feel energized. Your body experiences a heat flash, and your blood pressure increases. That is the body's reaction. What goes on in your mind is the next query. Test volunteers had MRIs done, and the researchers assessed their capacity to make decisions and use language when they were and weren't furious.

It has been confirmed that people's response time to linguistic stimuli increases when angry. This implies that even the smallest words spoken to you can rapidly make you snap. For example, when you're furious, trigger phrases like your narcissistic mother's derogatory statements can set you off right away and make you violent.

That is advantageous in some situations. However, scientists have also discovered that anger lowers your ability to make decisions and use other high-level cognitive functions. This implies that if you harbor or hold onto your anger for an extended period, you can end up trapped in your predicament.

You are stuck on the thing that enraged you and are not progressing. Harboring anger can impede your ability to move forward in life. It also keeps the wounds from narcissistic abuse from healing.

It's All Right to Feel Furious with Yourself

Some women experience self-loathing and resentment after growing up with narcissistic mothers. They are upset with themselves for succumbing to their mother's deceptive tactics. Some criticize themselves for being ignorant; this is their adjective of choice. In the end, that encourages their inner critic.

You should be aware that it's acceptable to be upset at yourself. It's a normal reaction. The question now is, how do you handle it?

Anger within the Framework of the Bereavement Process

We discussed anger in the last chapter as a phase of our moments of sadness or a component of the mourning process. In these situations, anger plays a role in our final healing from abuse.

Anger enables you to rediscover your uniqueness and ability to experience or recognize your emotions. A daughter whom a narcissistic mother raised may feel that she is no longer unique. She believes her sole mission is to make her mother happy and respected.

Every kind deed she performs in this circumstance raises her mother's profile.

However, each time she behaves inappropriately, such as throwing a fit or acting rudely, her mother is embarrassed and degraded.

Anger allows you to let go of internal tensions. You reject those justifications and announce your existence to everyone, even your mother. You let the world know you are a living, breathing human with unmet wants. In this situation, anger serves as a self-defense mechanism.

Chapter 8: Getting Kids Out of the Hands of a Narcissistic Ex

You will continue to face a lot of difficulties after divorcing a narcissist. These issues increase in difficulty when children are involved. Your kids will require assistance in overcoming the harm that their narcissistic parent has inflicted, as well as learning how to handle divorce. Living with a narcissist is never simple, and it negatively affects your kids. To ensure they lead healthy and rewarding lives, they must learn various coping and healing techniques.

Numerous popular pieces of advice are offered to parents going through a divorce with kids; sadly, those of you who divorced a narcissist will not find success or relevance in these words. It's nearly hard to co-parent with a narcissist. Most of the time, your goal will be to lessen confrontation. By now, you should be aware that narcissists enjoy drama and will stop at nothing to agitate you or your kids to maintain their power and manipulation games.

You want to shield your kids from the cruelty perpetrated by narcissists. Refusing to interact with them is one of the greatest ways to achieve this, particularly if their actions are wrong. The attention that a narcissist seeks, whether it be positive or bad, is what matters to them. Disengaging will effectively close the opportunity and benefit you and your kids.

It can be frightening to stop interacting with a narcissist. It should be simple in theory, but as you are well aware, dealing with a narcissist never comes easily. It can get worse when they figure out what you are doing. They can get agitated. Standing your ground is the wisest course of action. The narcissist will eventually go on to another victim after realizing they cannot force you to engage in combat. It may take a while, so you must exercise patience and perseverance.

You must bear in mind that you should have as few conversations as possible with your narcissistic parent to maintain harmony and strive to withdraw from them. You will need to discuss issues about the children with them, but you do not have to discuss anything else. Additionally, remember that staying in touch with your former partner does not require face-to-face conversation.

In today's environment, there are many ways to contact someone without speaking a word. Many methods exist to communicate with the kids without speaking via text, email, and social media. A narcissist will try their hardest to use words to control you when you speak with them. For this reason, it will be beneficial to avoid having actual talks. It keeps you safe and gives you time to process your feelings so you don't lose your cool when they say something offensive or terrible.

When contacting their children, the narcissistic parent will need to have at least one phone number on file. They essentially just need that phone number. Don't give your private number away to anyone to save yourself more hassle. You can even set up a different email address to ensure that they are just contacting you in one particular location. This may lessen the drama that the narcissist always tries to create.

It is beneficial for you and your ex to communicate mostly via email for several reasons. It allows you time to evaluate the material before responding if the narcissist decides to turn nasty in an email. It also provides concrete proof of what your former partner is saying, which may be useful if you must reapply to appear in court.

In addition, it gives you a record of any agreements, schedule modifications, or other information that a court would require if your ex tries to cause serious issues.

It will benefit your kids if you and the narcissistic parent don't communicate too much. It won't damage them to hear you quarrel, and they won't be exposed to the nonsensical things your ex says. So, keeping them as far away as possible is in everyone's best interest.

One of the most important things you should prioritize when caring for injured children and assisting in their healing is your well-being. You will likely need to concentrate on healing if you have managed to escape the abuse that a narcissist brings into your relationship. You can be a stronger role model for your children if you are internally healthier.

Support groups and counselors should be utilized. Look for a support group that addresses the abuse that narcissists engage in, especially while searching for one. Support groups can help you understand how to set and stick to limits. This can assist you in maintaining your attention on both your own and your children's healing.

Reducing conflict should be the first goal of any parent.

Ensuring your children feel empowered and validated will come in second. Narcissists treat children in the same way that they treat everyone else. Unless the court rules that the situation is unsafe for the children, you won't be able to halt this.

Protecting your kids from the harmful actions of their narcissistic parents is nearly impossible.

Though it may seem like the ideal idea to keep them apart from the other parent, children want the attention of both parents. Even though one of you doesn't healthily return their affection, your kids still love you both. They must see their other parent and come to their conclusions about them. Seeing your kids suffer from the devastation that a narcissist can inflict is incredibly painful, but you have to walk back. Interfering will probably cause more harm than benefit. Because they don't understand why you would break up their relationship with their other parent, you can even have children who hate you. As difficult as it may be, you have to step back and let them discover their narcissistic parent for themselves.

You are in charge of the relationship between you and your children, even when you don't influence your kids' other parent much.

Whenever you feel inspired to take action, decide to be their ardent advocate and champion. Permit them to talk to you about anything and acknowledge the struggles and issues they are expressing. You must be the one to assist them in staying grounded since their narcissistic parent will manipulate and give them lies, warping their reality. You must use caution when listening to your kids and learning about their experiences to avoid disparaging their other parents. You may keep things neutral and straightforward while still providing your kids with the required validation and support. Use neutral phrases like, "I'm sure it doesn't feel good to hear that," or "I'm sorry you experienced that." Additionally, you should take pride in that none of the actions displayed by the other parent are related to them. They are not at fault. Children who are attempting to recover from divorce and the trauma that the narcissistic parent inflicts on them will also find structure to be quite beneficial. You can keep people in this reality by giving their life structure.

How Do Victims Of Narcissism Get Selected?

Narcissists typically seek out a very certain kind of individual to target as their victims. But since they are easily accessible, parents who suffer from narcissism are more likely to select their children as victims. They are also readily molded and lack a strong sense of right and wrong. These kinds of characteristics make it simple for a narcissist to mold their kids so they can constantly take care of their requirements. If the narcissist is someone else in your life, on the other hand, they need to go out and find other people who share their characteristics. Although narcissists can harm a wide range of people, some personality types are more susceptible than others. Let's examine the personality qualities that narcissists usually seek in their victims to help you defend yourself from narcissists in the future.

Compassion

A strong sense of empathy is one of the most essential qualities that a narcissist seeks in a potential partner. People who lack empathy will not provide narcissists with a lot of resources, attention, or praise. They have to pick victims who exhibit great empathy since they are not very empathic. For the narcissist to feel in charge and powerful, they need the gasoline that these people can provide. If not, they will turn away from praise and attention and look for another source.

Human empathy is utilized to take power away from victims in an abusive cycle. The narcissist depends on your capacity to view things from their "perspective" even while you are the victim of their abuse. This allows them to keep the cycle of abuse going. People with high levels of empathy are the perfect target for narcissists to manipulate to arouse sympathy following violent events. This explains why narcissistic mothers find it easy to manipulate youngsters. Because of their innate empathy, they will invent justifications and reasons to maintain the presence of a mother figure in their lives.

Because they know that sympathetic people would justify or condone their abusive behavior, narcissists rely on their ability to provide their victims with a sob story or a phony apology to make up for the abuse. Mothers, in particular, who are narcissistic, depend on their victims' capacity for empathy and forgiveness—even in the face of repeated abuse. By appealing to the empathy of their victims, narcissists can escape responsibility for all of their activities. Because they experience a great deal of remorse when they witness the narcissist being punished, sympathetic people frequently regret their choices to make them accountable for their abusive actions.

Being diligent

Consciousness is among the most desirable personality qualities that narcissists seek out. Conscientious people naturally care about other people's well-being and try to fulfill their commitments. People who possess this trait tend to base their decisions on their conscience. Thus, they project their values and views onto others—in this case, a narcissist—and believe that the narcissist would act in the same way. Because they are aware that these people frequently worry about the needs and feelings of others, narcissists are naturally drawn to these kinds of people.

Narcissists can take advantage of this trait to further their interests. Conscientiousness is typically developed in children of narcissistic parents due to the constant pressure to put others before themselves. Children with narcissistic parents may grow up to be "people pleasers" because their coping mechanism was to only please their parents to keep them safe from violence or conflict.

Narcissists are aware that someone conscientious will view them favorably and presume the best. They are aware that these individuals frequently give them second opportunities and are only concerned with taking care of the narcissist's wants, even at the price of their well-being wellbeing. These are the kinds of persons that narcissists typically choose for romantic relationships. They think a very conscientious person would want to care for them in every way, even if it puts them in danger.

Adaptability

The bond between the victim and the narcissist is reinforced by those who are resilient and quick to recover from traumatic experiences. Abused people are prime targets for narcissists because they need someone who can bear a significant deal of suffering without giving up. Resilient victims may be more able to recognize danger and abuse because they have experienced it before.

Still, they are also less willing to give up on the narcissist even after experiencing repeated instances of abuse.

Honesty

Strong moral principles are attractive to narcissists because they are trustworthy and will honor their commitments. Narcissists can take advantage of several qualities that people with integrity possess. Those with integrity fear betrayal or "retaliation," even though most narcissists don't feel guilty about hurting their victims. Although these people's honesty will help them in relationships with other empathic people, narcissists might take advantage of it to undermine their self-worth and trust.

Emotionality

Narcissists find great attraction in sensitive and profoundly loving people because they may use a lot of flattery and praise to manipulate their victims. At the beginning of their relationship, narcissists may idealize their victims to gain their trust by providing for their emotional requirements. They would deliberately instill happy memories so that their victims can fantasize and reflect on past instances of abuse. Narcissists like manipulating their victims' emotions because they know how to boost their self-esteem and maintain their belief in their benefits, even during abusive episodes.

Chapter 4: Various Narcissistic Personality Types

Know which of your traits are narcissistic? Aside from researchers, doctors, psychologists, and psychotherapists, very few people know all the varieties. In the eyes of the general public, a narcissist is just that—a narcissist. When dealing with one, types truly don't matter.

However, how a narcissist expresses themselves and how to handle them depends on the kind of narcissist.

We've now read about their sense of entitlement—that they should receive preferential treatment—and their sense of superiority over other people. They live in a dream world where they think they are superior to others regarding prosperity and power. We now know that it is also a result of their fears and that, at their core, they have extremely flimsy egos and will stop at nothing, even if it means lying. The characteristics of an NPD individual are completed by their lack of empathy, how they take advantage of others, and how they utilize people by using them for their purposes.

Nonetheless, there is a spectrum of narcissism. Not every individual with NPD fits within the same mold. There are three main categories of narcissists, and each has a unique combination of characteristics. Each has unique strategies for defending their fragile egos, yet some may have the same goals.

Interestingly, some sub-categories represent how the features may be displayed to others within the three main types the researchers identified.

Researchers and mental health experts can get confused from time to time. When describing the same type, different labels are frequently applied. Furthermore, even when two categories are describing the same kind or sub-type, different labels are applied to them.

It has become challenging to identify and comprehend the type of narcissist being discussed because of all these variances in narcissist types and sub-types (Milstead, Ph.D., Kristen, 2018).

Five Sub-Types and Three Types

Researchers have identified three main categories of narcissism and five subtypes of narcissism. Different scholars use different terms to identify them independently. They explain their relationships with each other in detail.

Three Main Narcissistic Types

Traditional Narcissist

Grandiose, exhibitionist, or highly functional narcissists — When most people hear the word "narcissist," they typically think of "typical narcissists." These people are narcissists; they boast about their accomplishments, clamor for attention, and feel entitled to special treatment. They also want others to flatter and praise them. The most blatant kind of narcissism is this one.

They consider themselves the most significant and powerful individuals of all time. By bragging about their achievements, they hope to inspire admiration or jealousy in others.

This kind of narcissist is capable of charm and charisma. Their aspirations can align with the achievements they take great pride in, drawing you into their adoring orbit.

They become bored if the talk shifts its attention from them to someone else. They dislike having anyone else take center stage. They rarely enjoy sharing the spotlight with anyone else since they believe they are the most important topic.

Ironically, they believe they are better than everyone they encounter, even though they want to be acknowledged and valued.

Negative narcissists

Toxic narcissists This is the kind of narcissist that is extremely manipulative and exploitative, with behaviors that are not only antisocial but also often associated with psychopathic and sociopathic traits. This kind of narcissist differs from the descriptions of the other two main categories, susceptible and classical, in that they often exhibit a vicious streak.

Their main objective is to dominate and control others; to do this, they will lie, cheat, steal, and use aggression; they have no regrets about what they do. They could take pleasure in other people's pain.

Easily Fallible Narcissists

Compensatory, fragile, or hidden narcissists: Though they dislike being in the spotlight, they feel better than other people they meet. They detest it. Generally speaking, they prefer being around unique individuals to receiving special attention for themselves. They use extreme generosity or pleas for pity to win others' attention and appreciation to boost their self-esteem (Milstead, Ph.D., Kristen, 2018).

Vulnerable narcissists can emotionally deplete others. This is because they are also highly sensitive in addition to their emotional demands. They want other people to think of them as the ideal creatures that they are.

Because their fantasy life, which they believe they are entitled to, doesn't align with their actual reality, narcissists of this sort are more likely to experience depression.

Acknowledge the myths around mental illness and personality problems. Seeking attention, some people harm themselves—either by actual harm or by threats of harm. Realize that narcissists who threaten to kill themselves to gain attention are considered vulnerable.

They seldom follow through on the threat, though.

Ineffective communication: The most common way manipulative families communicate with each other is through triangulation. Instead of just passing information from one person to another, the narcissistic parent usually involves someone else to guarantee that the information gets to its intended destination. The family members engage in mutual gossip, but nobody is ever addressed face-to-face. This style of communication generates distrust and conflict by generating a passive-aggressive attitude. Overt touch usually happens when someone is angry.

There is no hierarchy – In stable homes, there is usually a distinct parental hierarchy where parents provide their kids guidance, love, and light. This type of interaction does not occur in narcissistic families. Consequently, it is the children's responsibility to tend to their parents' needs.

Unable to accept emotional accountability: Selfish people are incapable of providing emotional support and acceptance for their children because they lack empathy and unconditional love. Rather than being kind and sympathetic, they are more severe and critical of their kids. For this reason, their kids wind up going above and beyond to satisfy their parents' needs for approval and affection.

Sibling rivalry: In stable households, siblings are frequently expected to be kind and close to one another. Sometimes, children raised by narcissists are forced into unhealthy rivalries with one another. It's common to distinguish between children who are and are not superior. A child might be favored above the others, and other children might be used as a convenient scapegoat for their parents' negative emotions. Typically, siblings raised in narcissistic homes become apart from one another.

"You're never going to be enough": Selfish parents frequently use this phrase to tell their kids that they are "not good enough" in several different ways. They might act as though it's true or tell their kids. Narcissists often behave in an arrogant, greedy, and self-deprecating manner. Usually, this self-loathing mentality is inherited by their kids.

Everything is centered on how certain people see manipulative parents and how they look. They convey to the outside world that their family is stable and robust. They also make their families put up a pleasant front. When growing up in this environment, kids frequently worry about what their peers, neighbors, and relatives will think of them. They fear that people will see their dysfunction and turn away from them.

Dynamics In Which The Narrator Is A Parent Or An Authority Figure

When a parent or other influential figure exhibits narcissism, it usually manifests as someone who is well-liked by the public. Most likely, this person works as a judge, attorney, doctor, or teacher. They can keep a good balance between their personal and work lives. Well, that's the appearance. But the majority of people are ignorant of the fact that this Superman is lying. In this instance, narcissism is the issue. Although others might admire them, their children might recall them as arrogant and prone to irrationality.

He or she is, in actuality, 'always correct,' and nobody is permitted to challenge that. You understand that even though many of his or her peers and coworkers genuinely appreciate him or her, they don't know them as you do. Yes, you do occasionally experience love, but it's usually unpredictable. You feel like you must tread carefully most of the time, and there's a lot of anger at home.

Instead of taking advantage of their kids, parents who are not narcissistic would return home to mentor and assist them. To satisfy their own needs, narcissistic parents control their children. For young toddlers who are still developing, this is quite hazardous. You can't comprehend as a baby that your parents' affection isn't reliable. They are always correct—but not because they are, per se, but because they must be. You are taught everything they say is true, so you must believe them completely.

Since they depend on their parents for support, kids don't question them. When a parent loses their temper with their child over something like a mistake, being interrupted, or not finishing their homework, the child could start to believe that they are the cause of the issue. They feel a great lot of terror while they are with their parents. The youngsters will realize they are not receiving the same level of care as other kids when they become older, and their minds expand from more exposure to the natural world. Growing up with narcissistic parents teaches many kids to avoid confronting them. They take this action to avoid reprisals for allegedly being "ungrateful." As a result, the kids learn to walk carefully around the violent adult, crossing their fingers that they won't get upset.

The dread of being alone or angry manipulates children who grow up in this environment. Frequently, the other parent either accepts it to avoid being the target of the aggression or leaves the situation because of the violence. If any of these situations seem similar to you, your parent is probably narcissistic.

Let's look at some of the most noticeable and distinctive characteristics of a parent who exhibits narcissism. First, this parent appears to be in good health from the outside. The controlling parent appears to have it all together to people who are not living there. They sit on the school board, have a great career, earn a good livelihood, and take their kids on field trips. They wave hello to all the other guardians as they drive them to hockey or gymnastics practice. Being appreciated and drawing admiring and envious stares from other parents is very important to this parent. They place a high importance on their appearance in terms of their general development and appearance.

A narcissistic parent or other authority figure's second characteristic is usually their extreme self-centeredness. This parent is more focused on taking care of herself than her child. Regardless of their age or number of children, he or she prioritize their personal needs and needs for attention and validation over all else. This conceited parent gets angry easily. They will become irate and snap at their kids if things do not go according to plan or if they do not receive the care they desire.

The fact that manipulative parents or authoritative figures are ALWAYS correct is another trait of them. They will not acknowledge that they could have been wrong and will not entertain the possibility that they ever did. It's highly unlikely that you'll hear them apologize. They get enraged and combative when you disagree with them or attempt to persuade them that they are incorrect. Lastly, one of this person's main traits is that they give you the impression that you should always exercise caution around them. Their children would knock themselves out to prevent a negative outburst since they doubt what they say due to their violent outbursts and unfriendly moments.

#: Be Aware Of Your Thoughts And Silence

Once more, all narcissistic actions stem from an inability to take offense. When something is said or done, it's not because it's offensive or untrue; rather, you take offense because your inner voice tells you that you should. Recall that feelings come from thoughts; thoughts come from emotions, which lead to reactions.

By becoming mindful of your inner monologue and thoughts, you can become more conscious of the times when your thoughts drive your actions and make you act domineering and manipulative toward family members and other people. Try to be more conscious of the thoughts that lead you to behave (or respond) in a way others could interpret as arrogant or self-absorbed.

The first step to controlling and then progressively conquering narcissism is to become aware of the internal and external acts, words, and behaviors that set you up to act or react narcissistically toward the people in your life.

Your ability to control your triggers will increase as you become more conscious. Additionally, by recognizing the triggers for your egotistical behavior toward family and friends, you can provide yourself with a brief opportunity to select a different, more compassionate response rather than a selfish one.

#: Take up meditation

As you will discover later, if you are aware of your triggers, one of the things you need to do is put a distance between the trigger and your reactions to overcome narcissism and cease being dominating in relationships.

You can select a more sympathetic response by establishing this brief interval between trigger and reaction. Regretfully, it is difficult to become conscious enough to separate triggers from your response, although it gets better with meditation.

There are various aspects to meditation.

However, you can utilize narcissism as a tactical tool to develop present-moment awareness, get a deeper understanding of oneself, and detach from situations by viewing them objectively.

It will become easier to control difficult emotions and to be thoughtful in your actions and reactions as you constantly practice meditation and develop the mental state of being able to stay aware of this moment without altering or reacting to it.

Furthermore, regular meditation practice can help you become more self-aware, which will help you understand the emotional traumas that contributed to the development of your narcissistic personality as well as the situations that set off narcissistic tendencies.

You can learn how to disassociate yourself from situations that make you react narcissistically by engaging in meditation practices. It will assist you in viewing them objectively as transitory circumstances, enabling you to recognize that you do not need to respond to every narcissistic impulse you encounter.

The space between impulse and reaction formed when you learn to watch impulses such as narcissistic wrath, unpleasant emotions, self-centeredness, arrogance, super-minded thinking, etc., without being judgmental or reactive provides you the freedom to choose your reaction. Because you can select a more empathic response after there is a pause, this control—the pause—might prove to be quite helpful in combating chronic narcissistic tendencies.

The best part of it all is that meditation not only enables you to relate to your ideas rather than react to them, but it also makes you conscious of the self-serving, narcissistic narratives you tell yourself.

You can have a closer relationship with the mental models you have constructed by being aware of these stories. When you know these models are not serving you as well as you would like, it becomes easy to choose a different model whenever the trigger for one model appears.

Luckily, it's not too difficult to practice meditation to become aware of your narcissistic mental models, identify situations in which they arise, and select a more appropriate reaction.

Note: You cannot become less of a narcissist by meditation alone. It merely heightens your awareness of who you are, what you do, how you react, and how others perceive you.

It assists you in identifying situations and triggers for when you are prone to act controlling or on the verge of engaging in narcissistic behaviors because it fosters instantaneous self-awareness. Because of this understanding and dedication to improving yourself, you can select a more constructive course of action or response to a stimulus.

To develop a deeper feeling of inner and outer awareness, you can use a guided meditation app like Headspace or Calm or do the following meditation technique for five minutes three times a day.

Sit comfortably; although lying down is an option, sitting is more pleasant. Maintaining the natural curvature of the back while sitting upright requires caution to avoid becoming overly rigid.

Shut your eyes (you can also look down) and take a few slow, deep breaths. These initial deep breaths aim to become aware of and relax the body on a physical, mental, and emotional level. Breathe into the places where you may feel any tightness or stress in your body. Take note of your emotional state of mind and mental condition, whether peaceful or tumultuous.

Pay attention to the breath. Take note of all you can regarding the inhalation and the feelings you experience while doing so. Recall that the goal of awareness-gaining meditation is observation rather than modification! Simply let your awareness rest on your breath and observe it without making any changes or reactions. Apply the same principle to the exhale! Focus your attention on it and take note of everything that may be observed about it.

When the thoughts stray from the subject, as they often do, take note of its new location, rest your attention there for a little while, and then return your attention to monitoring your breathing. You will become more self-aware the more attentive to your breath you become.

Extend your awareness after spending some time studying your breath. Pay attention to the sounds in your meditation area first and your thoughts. Observe them without any judgment.

Call to mind any traumas you believe are the main reasons for your narcissism and watch them without passing judgment since the purpose of this meditation is to gain insight into your narcissistic tendencies. Allow them to unfold in your thoughts as though they were narratives witnessed by an outsider.

Similarly, recall times when you know you are prone to acting manipulatively, controllingly, or egotistically, and consider the situations or events that set these behaviors off. Once more, remember to watch these occurrences objectively without seeking to alter anything.

Instead of acting narcissistically, consider how you would like to behave and continue repeating a mantra to prepare your mind for the behavioral shift. Let's say, for example, that you become enraged and act out when your partner does not inquire about your day. Consider your usual response to this scenario to employ meditation to prepare your mind for changing your behavior.

This time, though, because you're determined to alter your behavior, consider what you want to do instead, something constructive, and make it your mantra. Say, "Whenever my partner does not ask me about my day, I will take ten deep breaths," for instance, if you wish to focus on your relationship after taking a few relaxing breaths. I'll question her about her day and listen intently until I'm more at ease. You will establish a neurological link by priming your mind in this way, which will assist you in identifying the trigger that makes you act selfishly. You will remember to use the alternate behavior rather than the selfish one whenever the trigger arises due to the formation of this brain association.

As previously indicated, meditation is not a panacea for narcissism. Additionally, you must be dedicated to improving yourself if you want it to work and make you a better person—someone who is more understanding and sympathetic.

www.ingramcontent.com/pod-product-compliance
Lightning Source LLC
Chambersburg PA
CBHW052141110526
44591CB00012B/1809